HAPPY & GLORIOUS

First published in Great Britain in 2006 by Cassell Illustrated,
a division of Octopus Publishing Group Limited
2-4 Heron Quays, London E14 4JP

A CIP catalogue record for this book is available
from the British Library.

ISBN-13: 978-1-844034-80-2
ISBN-10: 1-844034-80-1

10 9 8 7 6 5 4 3 2 1

Research by Ian Harrison
Design by John Round

Printed in China

HAPPY & GLORIOUS

A CELEBRATION OF THE LIFE OF HM QUEEN ELIZABETH II

PHOTOGRAPHY ROBIN NUNN

CASSELL
ILLUSTRATED

Octogenarian John Handford recalls seeing Princess Elizabeth during the reign of George V, when her father was still Duke of York and only second in line to the throne after his brother Edward.

“ I have only seen The Queen in person once in my life. I was on holiday in Weston-super-Mare during one of those sunny summers we used to have in the early thirties, and it was announced in the local press that the Duke and Duchess of York were to make a visit to the town in the coming week, presumably to open a hospital or perform some other ceremonial function. In those days such occasions were a signal for everyone in the town to turn out to see the Royal visitors. My family were fortunate to have a first-floor hotel room on the Royal route, and we thus had a grandstand view. It was a beautiful day and the visitors were in an open-backed limousine where the Duke, in naval uniform, and his wife and two young daughters were very visible. Princess Elizabeth must then have been about eight years old and her sister, Princess Margaret Rose, about six. Their composure in this situation was remarkable, and although it didn't occur to anyone then that the elder of the little girls would one day be Queen, one can see today that her training for that role began early. ”

LONDON, ENGLAND
4 AUGUST 1988

The Queen outside Clarence House on the occasion of The Queen Mother's 88th birthday. Clarence House is named after William, Duke of Clarence, for whom it was built before he ascended the throne as William IV. It became the home of The Queen Mother after Elizabeth II's accession in 1952.

When magician Jack Stephens arrived for what he thought was a routine booking to perform 'table magic' for a lunch party, he was surprised to discover the identity of the guest of honour.

“ In 2003 I was booked to entertain with my close-up table magic at a private lunch party near Cheltenham, Gloucestershire, and I noticed a guest walk past me who looked remarkably like The Queen. I assumed that, as a novelty, the host had hired a lookalike Queen – imagine my surprise when I was told it WAS The Queen! The host said I was simply to treat Her Majesty's table like any other. And what fun it was too. One bit of patter I used was during a trick where I give the guests a chance to win a big cash prize. (They never do, of course, always ending up with a penny.) When The Queen's table won the penny I said, 'You will know it's yours Ma'am – it has your picture on it!' I also do balloon sculpturing. I don't know how to model a corgi, but I made the Queen a cute little pink poodle and I said to her, 'It's a corgi going to a fancy dress party – dressed as a poodle'. She was amused! I found The Queen a delight to entertain and, in fact, no different to any other diner at the function. I wonder still...did the corgi (poodle) ever make it home to Buckingham Palace? ”

WINDSOR, ENGLAND
23 APRIL 2005

The Queen watches a display of Aston Martin cars in the Quadrangle at Windsor Castle on St George's Day. St George has been associated with Windsor Castle for more than six centuries, since he was adopted as patron saint of England by King Edward III, who founded the Order of the Garter and St George's Chapel (within Windsor Castle), both c.1348.

The late Charles Davis sat in judgement over Princesses Elizabeth and Margaret in a theatrical sketch written and performed at Balmoral. His daughter Pat Wragg remembers her father telling her about it.

" The 'Tha Wha' Club was founded in March 1944 by members of the Fifth Battalion Manchester Regiment (TA) to entertain the troops with sketches and concerts. In autumn 1944 the Regiment was stationed at Balmoral and one evening Princess Elizabeth said that she and Princess Margaret wanted to join the club. The members wrote a sketch entitled 'The Trial of Princess Elizabeth and Princess Margaret', in which my father was to play a judge presiding over the trial of the Princesses for reckless riding. He said that the Princesses read their parts beautifully with just the right touch of humour, and that their singing was delightful. He also said that Princess Margaret was a very accomplished piano player. They performed to a packed audience of the Royal Family, off-duty soldiers, and members of the Balmoral staff. That autumn HM The Queen presented the Regiment with a silver cup inscribed on one side: 'Presented to the 5th Bn. The Manchester Regiment by HM Queen Elizabeth'. And on the other side:

'Tha Wha'
Balmoral 1944. "

PREVIOUS PAGES

BUCKINGHAM PALACE, ENGLAND
12 JUNE 1993

CAPE TOWN, SOUTH AFRICA
21 MARCH 1995

From the Palace balcony, The Queen and other members of the Royal Family watch the RAF flypast that traditionally follows Trooping the Colour.

The Queen and Nelson Mandela on a walkabout on Cape Town's waterfront. Mandela had been inaugurated as South Africa's first black President less than a year earlier, on 10 May 1994.

Avid royal-watcher Sheila Clark often travels hundreds of miles from her home town of Glasgow to see The Queen, and was rewarded in 2005 with a surprise personal encounter.

66 In February 2005 I travelled from Scotland with fellow royal-watcher Alan Morton to see Her Majesty make her annual visit to West Newton Church near Sandringham. On the Saturday afternoon we were in the small village of Wolferton when I spotted The Queen's Range Rover coming slowly towards us. I was totally unprepared for what happened next.

The car stopped and the passenger door opened. We went forward to the car and there was Her Majesty behind the wheel laughing and looking very relaxed. Her Majesty's opening remark was, 'I bet I know where you are going to turn up tomorrow.' She knows us both well. I told her we'd come especially to see her. We chatted about the village and the weather. How the meeting would have continued I have no idea as suddenly Her Majesty realised that she was in the middle of the road and another car wished to pass. She left, calling 'See you tomorrow.'

It was an amazing experience and a one-in-a-million chance but something I will remember forever. 99

WEST NEWTON, ENGLAND
6 FEBRUARY 2005

The Queen, her eyes revealing sadness behind her smile, leaves West Newton Church near Sandringham after attending an annual ceremony to commemorate the death of her father, George VI, and her accession to the throne.

HORSE GUARD'S PARADE, ENGLAND
12 JUNE 2004

The Queen and the Duke of Edinburgh ride in a barouche during Trooping the Colour, a
ceremony first performed in 1755 and acted out annually as a means of marking the
sovereign's birthday since 1805, during the reign of George III.

FREDERICTON, CANADA
11 OCTOBER 2002

The Queen outside Old Government House, the home and
office of the Lieutenant-Governor of New Brunswick.

When Kim Hill heard that The Queen was to visit Fredericton on her Jubilee tour of Canada, he was determined to be noticed…

66 I took along with me a large picture of The Queen – a picture which used to hang in the school classrooms of Canada. I thought The Queen might notice it and stop. Then…the moment of The Queen's arrival…she was radiant in her matching salmon-pink coat and hat. The assembled crowd was jubilant. As she approached, I held the picture up at chest height. As the Queen walked towards me, she noticed the picture and stopped. Well, I was so excited, I spoke before she did. Whoops! I bowed and said 'Good afternoon Your Majesty', to which The Queen replied, 'Good afternoon.' I explained the history of the picture. The Queen seemed genuinely interested and said 'Well, well…that's nice.' Next, HRH Prince Philip walked by, and in his casual style commented 'That's a long time ago.' The following Monday I received an e-mail containing an internet link and the question: 'Is this you?' I clicked on the link and there was a Canadian Press photo of me holding the picture of The Queen, while speaking with her! I instantly ordered an 11" x 14" copy of the photo, which I now proudly display in my home. 99

Windsor, England
14 May 2005

The Queen at the Royal Windsor Horse Show. Legend has it that the reason dogs are now banned from what was originally the Windsor Horse and Dog Show is that in 1943, the show's first year, a dog stole a chicken leg from King George VI's plate, prompting an outright ban that lasts to this day.

OPPOSITE PAGE

SANDRINGHAM, ENGLAND
3 AUGUST 1997

A toddler changes her mind about presenting flowers to The Queen Mother and runs away, almost getting under The Queen's feet.

ABUJA, NIGERIA
6 DECEMBER 2003

The Queen and the Duke of Edinburgh wave farewell to President Obasanjo as they leave Nigeria at the end of their four day visit to the country to attend a Commonwealth Heads of Government Meeting.

YORK, ENGLAND
14 JUNE 2005

The Queen rides round York racecourse prior to Royal Ascot, one of England's oldest race meetings. Royal Ascot was founded by Queen Anne in 1711 on the course she had established at Ascot Heath, near Windsor, but in 2005 the meeting was moved to the even older course at York (established 1709) because Ascot was undergoing redevelopment.

In 1951 Captain Peter J.A. Traves Royal Canadian Navy (Retd.), who was then a young midshipman, received an ancient royal privilege from The Queen, who was then a young Princess Elizabeth.

❝ In November 1951 I was a midshipman serving on HMCS *Ontario*, a Canadian light cruiser. We were taking HRH Princess Elizabeth and the Duke of Edinburgh on a cruise around Canada and in Charlottetown we midshipmen attended a dance at the yacht club. On returning on board we were told that our leave was stopped for a month because we were considered to have been 'necking on the dance floor,' when we had in fact been dancing cheek-to-cheek.

Afterwards my best friend asked me if I had ever heard of royal clemency, saying that the King could get you off hanging! Later he said to Her Royal Highness, 'Ma'am, I request royal clemency for nine midshipmen who are under stoppage of leave for necking on the dance floor in Charlottetown.' She looked a little bemused and turned to the Duke who said, 'Go away and we will think about it.' The next day, over the ship's sound system, it was announced that Princess Elizabeth, in the name of the King, was pleased to grant royal clemency to all officers and men in HMCS *Ontario*. A large cheer went up and the midshipmen were saved. ❞

REGINA, CANADA
20 MAY 2005

The Queen at the opening of the Government House Heritage Property Centennial Project in Regina, a new addition to Government House which has been built to facilitate tours focussing on the role of constitutional monarch in the province. Her Majesty dedicated the 'Queen Elizabeth II Wing' and toured the new facilities.

Rob Plowright has dual nationality, having been born in Canada to English emigrant parents. In 1995-96 he participated in a teaching exchange and taught at Wilton Church of England Middle School near Salisbury.

" In May 1996, while I was residing in Salisbury, my neighbour invited my wife Hilary, my two sons, and I to The Queen's visit to the military base in Wilton. The Queen and Prince Philip had come to unveil a plaque and inspect the troops. After the inspection and unveiling, Her Majesty was on her way to the Warrant Officer's Mess for tea. My two boys were waving Canadian flags, and The Queen came over to where we were standing. After asking William and James, 'Are you really Canadian?' she conversed with them about British Columbia and their thoughts on England.

She then began a conversation with me, about the differences between teaching in Canada and in England. We were amazed at her knowledge and genuine interest as she inquired about our experiences. She was so open and friendly, which really moved me. She put us all at ease with her relaxed manner and left us in awe. I have always been proud of my British heritage, but this made it all so real to me and has made 'God Save the Queen' that much more meaningful. "

SASKATOON, CANADA
19 MAY 2005

The Queen at the University of Saskatchewan, after visiting the university's internationally renowned research facility known as the Canadian Light Source Synchrotron (CLSS). After the visit to the CLSS, Her Majesty made a walkabout among the people of Saskatoon.

Twenty-year-old Rafael Cruz flew from his home in Seattle, USA, to see the Royal Couple during their 2005 state visit to Canada, and succeeded in presenting Her Majesty with a particularly apt gift.

“ It was 24 May 2005 when I first saw Her Majesty The Queen, outside Government House in Edmonton, Alberta. The day before I had bought a little present for The Queen – a small puppet moose. I arrived at around 7am at Government House to get a prime spot. Finally at 11.10am Her Majesty began to make her way to Government House but just as she went by me a journalist stopped in front of me, so I was unable to give her my present. Luckily, just a few seconds later, The Hon. Ralph Klein, Alberta's Premier, passed by. I shouted his name, and he took my moose for The Queen. To my disappointment, I saw him giving it to a lady-in-waiting, but later I found out that The Queen had indeed noticed my gift.

After The Queen had gone into Government House I ran down to Alberta's Legislature to see her again. During her walkabout I was able to ask The Queen if she had received my moose. The Queen graciously replied: 'So, you are the one who gave it to me.' I was so excited that I shouted 'I love you, your Majesty' so many times that I recollect over-hearing someone stating: 'Wow, I think someone is going crazy here.' ”

EDMONTON, CANADA
24 MAY 2005

The Queen arriving at the Northlands Coliseum for a dinner hosted on behalf of the Canadian Government by the Prime Minister, the Right Honourable Paul Martin.

As Ladies' National Showjumping Champion and a member of the British showjumping team from 1960 to 1976, Judy Crago had no difficulty in finding things to talk about when she met The Queen at the Montreal Olympics.

" My husband Brian was in the Australian Olympic Equestrian team in 1956 and 1960, and he met The Queen on several occasions – notably on the *Britannia* when Her Majesty hosted a party for the visiting Australian team who came over to England to train before the Games.

I also met her several times at various equestrian events, and my family and I spent a week in close proximity to the immediate Royal Family during the Montreal Olympic Games in 1976 when Princess Anne was in the British Three Day Event team. We were invited to an event hosted by the Queen for the British equestrian teams and Her Majesty was in her element. She has tremendous enthusiasm for all equestrian activities and a vast knowledge of the different disciplines, and on this occasion she immediately put us all at ease and engaged us in animated conversation about the horses and riders from the teams competing in the Games. Her sense of humour and fun are well known, but it is not until you meet her that this becomes apparent. We all felt it was a great honour and a privilege to meet her. "

WINDSOR, ENGLAND
12 MAY 2005

The Queen at the Royal Windsor Horse Show, Britain's largest outdoor equestrian show. The show was founded as the Windsor Horse and Dog Show in 1943 by Count Robert Orssich and Mr Geoffrey Cross as a means of raising money for the war effort.

PARIS, FRANCE
6 APRIL 2004

The Queen arrives at St Eustache Church, where she is met by a priest whose hat is blown off by the strong wind. The Eglise St Eustache was built from 1532-1640 and dominates the modern gardens and arcades of Les Halles, an area which, similarly to London's Covent Garden, was a wholesale fruit and vegetable market from medieval times until the 1960s.

OTTAWA, CANADA
14 OCTOBER 2002

The Queen visits the Royal Canadian Mounted Police Equestrian Centre during her Golden
Jubilee tour of Canada. The RCMP have held a special place in The Queen's affections since
they presented her with what became her favourite mount, the mare Burmese, which until
1986 Her Majesty traditionally rode at Trooping the Colour.

Jean Godfrey (née Leon) used to play with Princesses Elizabeth and Margaret at Englemere Wood orphanage near Ascot. The Reverend Denis Godfrey relates his wife's memories of those happy occasions.

"Jean was one of several orphans living at Englemere Wood until the Grenville House orphanage was made available. Between 1941 and 1944, at both locations, King George and Queen Elizabeth attended Board meetings of the Home. On these occasions they brought Princesses Elizabeth and Margaret who played with the orphans of their age group. Jean is one week older than Margaret, so most of her time was spent with her. She remembers that both Princesses were full of life and enjoyed their games, particularly skipping and nature walks. Jean says that they seemed perfectly normal children with the same likes and dislikes as they had. The girls were permitted to call them Lisbeth and Margaret. After the orphans moved to Grenville House, they had very little opportunity to play with the Royal children, although they saw them from time to time when the King visited. Jean and some of the older orphans also spent quite some time with the Princesses Marie Louise and Helena Victoria, who lived in Englemere House and hosted sessions where the children knitted for the forces."

HOUNSLOW, ENGLAND
15 OCTOBER 2004

The Queen and the Duke of Edinburgh arrive to open Phase 2 of the development of the Sikh temple Gurdwara Sri Guru Singh Sabha in Hounslow. Her Majesty is met by Bymr Gurcharan Singh Chatwal, President of the Gurdwara, who presents her with a garland.

FALMOUTH, ENGLAND
1 MAY 2002

The Queen enjoys the first day of her Golden Jubilee tour of the UK. Her Majesty
arrived at Falmouth Docks Station in the Royal Train and made her way to the new
National Maritime Museum Cornwall, where she performed her first official duty of
the tour: launching a new lifeboat from the museum's harbourside pontoon.

VANCOUVER, CANADA
6 OCTOBER 2002

The Queen meets the opposing captains before dropping the puck for a
ceremonial face-off at the start of an exhibition ice hockey match between
the Vancouver Canucks and the San Jose Sharks.

An organist and choirmaster with more than 70 years' service to the Church, Eric Stephenson met The Queen after being chosen as a Maundy Money recipient in 2005.

❝ On 24 March 2005 at Wakefield Cathedral a total of 158 men and women were recipients of the Maundy Money, selected because of the Christian service they have rendered to the Church and the community. My wife June and I had an early start, driving to join other recipients at the Cedar Court Hotel before being transported to the Cathedral. The Maundy Service included a lesson read by the Duke of Edinburgh, and afterwards Her Majesty and the Lord High Almoner distributed the Maundy Money and congratulated me on my long service to the Church. The Maundy Money (79 pence in silver coins, being the 79 years of The Queen's age) is contained in a white goat-skin bag and there was an extra award this year: a red goat-skin bag bearing within a pure silver £5 coin commemorating the 200th anniversary of the Battle of Trafalgar. After the service we returned to the Cedar Court to enjoy a meal presided over by the Bishop of Pontefract and to reflect on a day the memory of which I will cherish for the rest of my life. ❞

JASPER, CANADA
22 MAY 2005

The Queen arrives for a Sunday morning church service
during her tour of Alberta.

WINDSOR, ENGLAND
15 JUNE 1998

The Queen arriving for the annual service of the Order of the Garter.
Britain's oldest and most prestigious order of chivalry, the Order of the
Garter was founded by Edward III in 1348.

When Jack Binks, MBE, met The Queen in his capacity as the last Mayor of the Borough of Morley, he was struck by her delicate sense of humour.

" In 1974 I was invited to a reception at St James's Palace for all the Mayors and Lord Mayors in England, and (because they knew each other) all the people from the West Riding of Yorkshire assembled in one part of the room. When The Queen came in she shook hands with me and said, 'Where are you from, Mr Mayor?' and I said, 'From Morley, Your Majesty, in your very loyal West Riding. You may remember you had a very successful tour there after the Coronation.' 'Ah, yes,' she said, 'everybody was so kind.'

She moved on, shaking hands with everybody else, but then she came back to me and she said, 'Mr Mayor, tell me: why do all you West Riding people gang up in one corner of the room?' 'Well,' I said, 'the truth of the matter is, Ma'am, that we're the only people here who can understand each other.' And with a twinkle in her eye and broad smile she said, 'There's far more truth in that than you realise!' which I thought showed her great sense of humour because she wasn't frosty; she was ready for a laugh about anything. "

WINDSOR, ENGLAND
11 JUNE 1989

Her Majesty presents The Queen's Cup polo award at Windsor. The annual Queen's Cup competition was founded half a century ago by the Duke of Edinburgh, encouraged by his uncle Lord Mountbatten, and is the premier event in the polo calendar.

EDMONTON, CANADA
24 MAY 2005

As she leaves the Alberta Legislature The Queen smiles but
gives a wide berth to a cow brought along to the royal occasion by
Tracey and David Morey of Rochester, just north of Edmonton.

The Queen on a walkabout in the Market Square. Romford has long-standing royal connections, and owes its growth from a Roman barracks into a market town to its proximity to an ancient royal palace at Havering. Henry III granted Romford market its royal charter in 1247 and Henry IV granted permission to build the original Church of St Edward in 1406.

ROMFORD, ESSEX
6 MARCH 2003

The Queen on a walkabout in the Market Square. Her Majesty agreed to visit the
London Borough of Havering after the Mayor, Peter Gardner, wrote to her expressing
his disappointment that Havering had not been included in The Queen's Golden Jubilee
tour of East London.

Former Royal Marine Rodney Spinks, now in his sixties, remembers being in the presence of The Queen as the proudest moment of his military career.

" On 23 July 1964 over two thousand serving and retired members of the Royal Marines assembled on the lawns of Buckingham Palace to celebrate the Tercentenary of the Royal Marines (1664–1964). HM Royal Marines Band, a Guard of Honour and distinguished guests from many nations all gathered to show Her Majesty the Corps in its modern setting. The weather was perfect for the day and Her Majesty looked lovely wearing a pastel pink dress. She inspected the Guard of Honour and then took the Salute. The parade was stood at ease and Her Majesty then addressed the Marines present, ending with the words: 'I send my best wishes to all Royal Marines past and present and to their families on this 300th anniversary of the foundation of Britain's Sea Soldiers.' A copy of the speech was later given to all on parade. I was there and it was the proudest moment of my 11 years' service in HM Royal Marines to have been near and seen Her Majesty. I have this speech framed and hanging on my wall in my home. It's my pride and joy. "

BANDAR SERI BEGAWAN, BRUNEI
18 SEPTEMBER 1998

The Queen in the capital of Brunei on the second day of her State visit.

St Paul's Cathedral
14 July 2000

The Queen leaves St Paul's after attending the annual service of the Order of St Michael and
St George. The order was founded in 1818 by the Prince Regent on behalf of George III.

WINNIPEG, CANADA
8 OCTOBER 2002

The Queen meets members of the Pembroke Welsh Corgi Association of Canada at The
Forks. The name describes the junction of the Red and Assiniboine rivers, an ancient
Aboriginal meeting place that is now a modern leisure and commercial centre.

Dorothy Ridd was the event coordinator for The Queen's visit to The Forks in Winnipeg, during which her mother-in-law Kathleen had a moving encounter with The Queen.

66 The backdrop for Her Majesty's visit was the Assiniboine River and the grassy terraces overlooking the Historic Port at The Forks – an ideal location for the public to gather to catch a glimpse of Her Majesty and Prince Philip. My mother-in-law, Kathleen ('Kitty') Ridd, was standing at the entrance in the lower patio with me and her two great-grandsons Clay and Cole. The Queen looked directly at me as she approached our group and I called out to Her Majesty telling her that my mother-in-law was a British war bride. The Queen stopped directly in front of Kitty, took her hand and held it for a moment while they spoke. I could feel Kitty trembling. This emotional moment brought tears to her eyes as well as to those in close proximity. The Queen then proceeded down the steps, stopping to chat with people along the way. After The Queen had passed by us one of her ladies-in-waiting stepped up to Kitty and presented her with a long stem rose. She treasures the rose to this day, along with numerous photos capturing the memory of this special moment. 99

BONN, GERMANY
19 OCTOBER 1992

The Queen attends talks and lunch at Villa Hammerschmidt with President Richard von Weizsacker at the start of her state visit to Germany. Villa Hammerschmidt was the official residence of the German President from 1951 to 1994.

Michael Jackson, LVO, has worked on three of The Queen's visits to the Canadian province of Saskatchewan, the last two as Royal Visit Coordinator.

" It is evident that Her Majesty is very comfortable in her role as Queen of Canada, which is quite separate from her roles as Queen of the United Kingdom or Head of the Commonwealth. I am always struck by her ready wit, vivacity and keen interest in everyone she meets and everything she sees. My most recent memories are of The Queen's May 2005 visit to Saskatchewan for the province's centennial. The Royal Couple flew directly to Regina from London immediately after the state opening of the UK Parliament and we were all astounded at how they promptly and energetically launched into another round of activities – despite, as Her Majesty told me, it being '1.30 in the morning our time.' Her Majesty constantly pulls off a *tour de force*: at one and the same time she is an internationally admired and respected icon of democracy, and a warm, sympathetic human being gifted with a delicious sense of humour. Canada is very fortunate indeed that this remarkable lady is our Queen and symbol of our sovereignty. "

REGINA, CANADA
17 MAY 2005

The Queen with Chief Alphonse Bird of the Federation of Saskatchewan Indian Nations after a ceremony paying tribute to First Nations veterans during Canada's 'Year of the Veteran'. The event was held at First Nations' University of Canada.

Ken Rollin met The Queen at Wembley Stadium after the 1960 Rugby League Challenge Cup Final, at which Her Majesty presented the Cup to Ken's team, Wakefield Trinity.

" It was 1960, Wakefield vs Hull – I scored the first try in about two minutes and we went on to win 38–5. The Queen presented the medals and she spoke to each of us to say congratulations, you played well. The only thing I can remember clearly, because when it's happening it goes so quickly, is that her hand was so small that it was quite remarkable. I always remember that particular detail.

When the competition started in February we were playing at St Helens and we were told that if we could win that match we were good enough to reach the final – 'and by the way The Queen and the Duke of Edinburgh will be there.' So the motivation was there right at the beginning. On the day the teams were presented to the Duke at the beginning of the match and then Her Majesty presented the Cup at the end. Winning the Challenge Cup is the highlight of any Rugby League player's career but this was even more special because The Queen was there. "

EDMONTON, CANADA
23 MAY 2005

The Queen manages a smile despite the downpour that spoiled the Official Welcome to Alberta in the Commonwealth Stadium, Edmonton. Alberta became a Canadian Province in 1905, and as part of 'Alberta's 100th birthday party' The Queen and the Duke of Edinburgh witnessed the cutting of an enormous birthday cake before making an official walkabout.

ADELAIDE, AUSTRALIA
28 FEBRUARY 2002

The Queen meets past winners of the Adelaide Hills Kennel Club's top award, The
Queen's Trophy. Her Majesty is shaking hands with Mrs Cheryl Shepherd,
whose dog, Ch Bekaa Superspell, won the trophy in 1995.

CAIRNS, AUSTRALIA
1 MARCH 2002

The Queen visits the Royal Flying Doctor Service, which was established in 1928 as the first
comprehensive aerial medical organisation in the world and which still provides a vital
emergency and general health service for Australia.

BUCKINGHAM PALACE, ENGLAND
17 JUNE 1989

The Queen and other members of the
Royal Family on the Palace balcony
after Trooping the Colour.

In his role as Commander of the New Zealand Army's 3rd Land Force Group, Colonel Martin Dransfield, ONZM, hosted The Queen's visit to Burnham Camp in 2002.

“ The visit involved a traditional welcome by the Maori Culture Group, as part of which my children and other servicemen's children were proud to perform a waiata (traditional song). We hosted Her Majesty and the Duke of Edinburgh for lunch in the Officers' Mess, during which she was very attentive to our conversation and demonstrated a great sense of humour. After lunch she spoke with a large number of soldiers about their experiences in East Timor and aspirations for the forthcoming tour of operations. I vividly remember her tremendous abillity to put them at their ease by showing an interest in every soldier and impressing them with her knowledge of military matters.

My son Isaac (then aged 11) remembers The Queen as an 'impressive person who we were very proud to welcome to New Zealand. It was cool, a once in a lifetime experience.' My daughter Leah (then aged eight) remembers her as a 'beautiful lady in a bright coloured dress who smiled when we sang, but didn't wear a crown.' ”

SEOUL, SOUTH KOREA
22 APRIL 1999

The Queen meets veterans of the Korean War at a garden party held in their honour at the British Embassy. The Korean War was the first major armed conflict to be fought under the aegis of the United Nations, and brought the world to the brink of a third world war just five years after the second.

PARIS, FRANCE
5 APRIL 2004

The Queen at a State banquet at the Elysée Palace on the first night of her three-day State
visit to France to celebrate the 100th anniversary of the most recent revival of entente
cordiale: President Chirac reciprocated with a visit to Britain later in the year.

OSLO, NORWAY
31 MAY 2001

The Queen meets the people of Oslo outside the Town Hall. The British and Norwegian royal
families enjoy close ties, being blood relations – King Olav V of Norway, who reigned from
1957–91, was born at Sandringham and is the grandson of King Edward VII.

Derek Morgan, OBE, DL, first met The Queen when he was invited to Buckingham Palace to celebrate the millennium of the Shrievalty.

" I was High Sheriff of Mid-Glamorgan from 1988 to 1989, and in November 1992 a number of past and current High Sheriffs were invited to Buckingham Palace to meet The Queen and the Duke of Edinburgh. The reason for this honour was to celebrate the millennium of the Shrievalty, or office of Sheriff, which dates back to the 10th century. My wife Anne accompanied me to the Palace, where we were directed to one of several rooms set aside for the occasion. I was fortunate to be one of the past High Sheriffs from Wales chosen to be presented to Her Majesty and the Duke of Edinburgh. The Queen arrived early, with a severe cold, and she looked very sad because it was just three days after the great fire at Windsor Castle; it was also the night before she made her speech describing 1992 as her annus horribilis. The Queen and the Duke were most gracious, enquiring which county I had represented, and about my memories of my year in office. Despite her worries she spent a good deal of time with each of those presented and made it into a very special occasion indeed. "

NOTTINGHAM, ENGLAND
21 MARCH 1997

The Queen outside Nottingham Magistrate's Court during an awayday to the city. It was in Nottingham, in 1642, that King Charles I raised his standard, marking the start of the English Civil War.

ISLAMABAD, PAKISTAN
7 OCTOBER 1997

The Queen showing due respect to the
Muslim faith during a visit to the Shah
Faisal Mosque in the Pakistani capital.

CAIRNS, AUSTRALIA
1 MARCH 2002

The Queen at the Tjapukai Aboriginal Cultural Park, one of Australia's most popular tourist attractions. A success story that has eased racial tension, spurred Aboriginal self-determination and revived local Aboriginal language and culture, the Park provides a theatrical interpretation of Aboriginal culture to visitors from around the world.

PARIS, FRANCE
6 APRIL 2004

The Queen meets the crowds after visiting the Palais du Louvre during a
State visit to celebrate the 100th anniversary of the most recent revival of
entente cordiale – a phrase first coined in 1843 to describe friendly
relations between England and France and revived in 1904.

Gordon Johnson met The Queen in the mid-1970s, when he travelled to Buckingham Palace to receive an MBE.

" For many years I worked for the Metropolitan Water Board, so my MBE was for services to water. I was very surprised to receive the letter asking me if I'd like to receive the honour and requesting me not to tell anyone – which to be honest wasn't hard because I didn't want all my work colleagues ribbing me and accusing me of pulling their leg. When the day came, my wife and I were driven to Buckingham Palace in a Daimler and escorted into the ante-room next to where the ceremony was to take place. The recipients then lined up and entered the room, approaching Her Majesty to receive their honours. She was standing there flanked by two Ghurka officers and she spoke to each one of us, asking us what we'd done and thanking us for our service. I was very impressed by the way she managed to make us feel included, as though we were an important part of it all, rather than being on the outside of it. It was a great honour to receive my MBE from The Queen herself, and altogether a memorable day. "

LONDON, ENGLAND
4 AUGUST 1987

The Queen and her nephew David Linley outside Clarence House
during The Queen Mother's 87th birthday celebrations.

Kate Knowles, Head of Communications at the Dulwich Picture Gallery in London, found that meeting The Queen can have a strange effect on one's behaviour.

" When I knew The Queen was coming to reopen the Gallery in 2000, after it had been closed for 18 months for refurbishment, I rang up her office to ask what the protocol was. They said, no need to curtsey any more or bow; just a brief nod of the head is considered enough nowadays. So I sent an email round to my colleagues advising them of this. When I met The Queen I gave what I thought was a small inclination of the head. Later the photos appeared, and there I am in a deep curtsey – the sort I learned in ballet lessons when I was eight years old! "

PREVIOUS PAGES

SANDRINGHAM, ENGLAND
25 DECEMBER 1992

The Queen and Princess Margaret attend the traditional
Christmas Day service at Sandringham.

TAUPO, NEW ZEALAND
24 FEBRUARY 2002

The Queen leaves St Andrew's Church after attending
the Sunday morning service.

EPSOM, ENGLAND
1 JUNE 1988

The Queen at the Derby, flanked by
The Queen Mother and Princess Anne.
One of the 'English Classics', the
Derby was first run on 4 May 1780.

EDMONTON, CANADA
24 MAY 2005

Double portrait of The Queen at Edmonton's
Legislature Building.

LONDON, ENGLAND
1 AUGUST 2001

The Queen, standing in for The Queen Mother, who was ill at the time,
lays the foundation stone for the Memorial Gates in Constitution Hill.

Nathan Tidridge travelled to England from Waterdown, Ontario, to see The Queen, and was rewarded with a smile and a wave from the Royal Couple.

" Some friends and I travelled to London in 2002 for The Queen's Golden Jubilee Celebrations. We staked out our area on the Mall, and promptly decorated it with Canadian flags. We gave out nearly 1,000 Canadian flags that day before the parade, earning the nickname 'Little Canada' from the people passing by (we were even featured on the news a few times back home).

The night before the parade, The Queen was driven out to light a beacon in front of the Victoria monument. Just as The Queen and Prince Philip drove by, I leaned over and waved my Canadian flag – catching the eye of Her Majesty. The Queen saw the flag, got Prince Philip's attention, pointed and they both waved back to us. I got it all on film. The crowd erupted – and for the rest of the night 'Little Canada' was the centre of much celebration! Other Canadians heard about our luck, and the night was filled with visitors bringing us chocolate, blankets, and of course Canadian whiskey. "

EDMONTON, CANADA
25 MAY 2005

The Queen during a walkabout in Churchill Square on the last day of
her 2005 visit, hosted by the Mayor of Edmonton, His Worship Stephen Mandell.

OPPOSITE PAGE

OTTAWA, CANADA
13 OCTOBER 2002

The Queen arrives for dinner at the Canadian Museum of
Civilization, the country's national museum of human history.

CHRISTCHURCH, NEW ZEALAND
25 FEBRUARY 2002

The Queen visits Burnham Military Camp, where she meets
soldiers training for international peace-keeping duties.

A resident of Toronto, John Aimers founded the Monarchist League of Canada and has served as its Dominion Chairman since 1970.

" I first met The Queen at a media reception held at Government House, St John's, Newfoundland, in the summer of 1976. Her Majesty and the Duke of Edinburgh were travelling through Newfoundland, Saskatchewan and Alberta prior to Her Majesty's opening of the Commonwealth Games in Edmonton, Alberta. When I was presented to The Queen in my capacity as correspondent for *Monarchy Canada* (then the periodical of the Monarchist League of Canada), she smiled and said 'hello' – I was struck by how commanding her presence was despite her small physical stature. The Duke, standing next to her, also shook hands but drew me back as I tried to move on, booming – to The Queen's evident amusement as well as that of my journalist colleagues – 'What, are you in competition with us?' Unforgettable. "

TORONTO, CANADA
10 OCTOBER 2002

The Queen after a gala concert at the Roy Thomson Hall (RTH). It was Her Majesty's second visit to RTH, having attended a Royal Gala performance by the Toronto Symphony Orchestra there on 31 October 1984. Eighteen years later she returned to RTH for the Canadian Broadcasting Corporation's Golden Jubilee Gala.

When John and Maureen Allen went to see The Queen on a walkabout in Windsor they expected to be at the back of a large crowd of royal well-wishers, but suddenly found themselves eye-to-eye with Her Majesty.

" During The Queen's Golden Jubilee celebrations my wife Maureen and I read that The Queen was due to re-open the bridge between Windsor and Eton that had been closed for refurbishment. We decided to go along and see the event, particularly as The Queen and Prince Philip were due to do a walkabout through the pedestrianised area to the bridge.

Windsor was very crowded but we managed to find a small space at the front of the throng about half-way along the walkabout route. After a wait of about two hours (and a couple of false alarms) a large black limousine drew up about 50 yards from us. The crowd started to buzz with excitement and then we saw The Queen walking towards us. She stopped a couple of times and acknowledged the crowd, followed by Philip who also stopped and chatted to some people.

The Queen looked very relaxed and happy, and as she approached where we were standing she looked straight at us and I got a really nice photograph of her smiling beautifully. She and Philip passed by all too quickly. "

WINDSOR, ENGLAND
15 APRIL 1997

The Queen goes shopping in Windsor. The name of the town has been synonymous with British royalty since June 1917, when George V renounced his German name and titles, adopting Windsor as the family name.

Eric Clay, nicknamed 'The Sergeant Major', has been described as 'the most famous referee in the history of Rugby League'. He met The Queen twice, after refereeing the 1960 and 1967 Challenge Cup Finals at Wembley.

" It was a very great honour to actually meet The Queen on two occasions, and I felt very very lucky. The first was the 1960 cup final, when Wakefield Trinity beat Hull, and the second was the 1967 final when Featherstone Rovers beat Barrow. Of course it was a case of just being introduced to Her Majesty and saluting her and thanking her for the badge she gave me – there wasn't a great deal of talk with her, but it was absolutely wonderful to be in a position to meet her. The second time was the same sort of feeling; I was delighted it had happened to me, and I felt just as honoured and just as lucky. I thought she was a very fine lady and I was very proud to meet her – it's a wonderful feeling when you're there. "

NEW BRUNSWICK, CANADA
12 OCTOBER 2002

The Queen at Sussex Elementary School, where she 'planted' a virtual tree. Her Majesty did so pressing a button on a computer keyboard to initiate a programme replicating the planting and development of the Canadian national tree, a red maple.

Despite being told not to speak unless spoken to, actor Andrew Bolton couldn't resist asking The Queen the 'all-important question' when she attended a Jubilee performance of The Mousetrap.

"Coincidentally The Queen's Golden Jubilee and the record-breaking 50th year of The Mousetrap's continuous run fell in the same year, 2002. Feelers had been put out from the theatre to the Palace and finally the rumour was confirmed that Her Majesty and Prince Philip would be attending a special, invitation-only, gala performance on our anniversary night, Monday 25 November. After the performance we were hastily lined up on stage, then the curtain was raised and to the audience's delight, The Queen, followed by Prince Philip, was introduced to us one at a time. We had been instructed not to speak unless spoken to, but when my turn came at the end of the line, I couldn't resist asking, 'Did you guess who'd done it?' Her Majesty replied to the effect that no, she had no idea, but her husband had guessed.

We were all impressed by the charm and elegance of The Queen who looked radiant, exuding warmth. She is surprisingly small, as is Philip, who I would have guessed, before this night, to have been a slim six-footer. In a way, they looked like the grandma and grandad of the nation."

LONDON, ENGLAND
3 JUNE 2002

The Queen joins Sir Cliff Richard and other stars on stage at the end of the pop concert held at Buckingham Palace to celebrate her Golden Jubilee.

After lunch in Windsor Great Park, Phil and Mary Harrison were surprised to find themselves treading divots with The Queen at a polo match.

" One summer Saturday in the mid-1960s my wife Mary and I were travelling from the West into London and, as it was late morning, we were looking for a place for lunch. On an impulse we turned into Windsor Great Park and, after finding a meal, noticed that there was to be a polo match. Never having seen the sport before, we decided to watch and parked our car on the side of the pitch near the halfway line. On the opposite side was what looked like a small marquee and we joked about it being for The Queen. However, it was not long before we noticed the Royal Standard flying over the 'stand' and realised that she really was there.

At intervals in a game of polo spectators are asked to go on to the field to tread down divots and we joined in with the few others present on our side of the field. As we came near to the middle of the field it was clear that The Queen was doing the same, walking towards us from her side of the field whilst chatting amiably to a friend. She had two of her children with her and we clearly heard Princess Anne say 'Oh Annnndrew!' – but quite what he had done will forever remain a mystery to us! "

STRANRAER, SCOTLAND
10 AUGUST 1996

The Queen makes a poignant stop-off for an official visit during the last summer cruise of the Royal Yacht *Britannia*, which was launched by Her Majesty at Clydebank in 1953.

Mary Relph lives in a small village close to the Royal estate at Sandringham. For the last 60 years she has followed The Queen and collected Royal memorabilia and photographs.

66 At Christmas and New Year when The Queen stays in Norfolk I never miss seeing Her Majesty attend morning service at Sandringham Church. I am also there when The Queen goes to two other churches on the estate. I have given The Queen flowers on many occasions.

One of my favourite sightings of Her Majesty was when I travelled to the north of Scotland to see the Royal Family disembark from the Royal Yacht *Britannia* and be greeted by The Queen Mother on the quayside at Scrabster. Then they travelled to the Castle of Mey for tea. On one occasion, as The Queen was boarding *Britannia* to sail to Aberdeen on the way to Balmoral, I said, 'I hope you have a lovely holiday.' The Queen turned to me and said, 'You will be able to put your camera away now, won't you?'

I was at Balmoral on 6 August 2005 to see Her Majesty in her Land Rover, complete with headscarf and corgis. We were visiting the grounds when she recognised me and two friends and slowed down and gave us a lovely wave. She said, 'How did you know I was at Balmoral? I thought I got in here without anyone knowing.' The Queen knows I come from Norfolk and recognises me each time I see her. 99

MONTEGO BAY, JAMAICA
20 FEBRUARY 2002

During the first stop on her Jubilee Tour of the Commonwealth,
a radiant Queen admires the watercolour 'Radiance' by Janette Eyles.

**Dr Terry Ryan, Secretary of the Rehua Marae in Christchurch,
New Zealand, remembers The Queen's 2002 visit to this historic site.**

" We worked hard for months to ensure that the Royal visit was a success, and after the year's 'non summer' that day turned out to be 'out of the bag'. That morning, The Queen's New Zealand standard was raised at the entrance to the Rehua Marae: it is believed this was the first time the standard has flown at a marae (traditional Maori meeting place) anywhere in New Zealand.

The emphasis was on the old and young of all iwi and peoples. Some 400 children came from the local area. All were issued with a New Zealand flag, which they waved enthusiastically. There were also some 700 people at the Marae, all intermingled as one. Great was the excitement when The Queen's car arrived right on time at 11 o'clock. The karanga (call), the powhiri (welcome) and the karakia (prayers) culminated with The Queen's reply to the words of welcome. She spoke briefly in Te Reo, doing herself credit with her faultless pronunciation. When she had finished, all those present broke into a rendition of 'God Save The Queen' in Maori to honour her. It was judged a great day for a great lady, and one which had honoured a significant site in the history of Christchurch City. "

CHRISTCHURCH, NEW ZEALAND
25 FEBRUARY 2002

The Queen wears a traditional Maori cloak of feathers during a meeting with leaders of the
Ngai Tahu people at the Rehua Marae. In honour of her visit to the marae, Her Majesty wore
the cloak that she had been given on her Coronation tour of New Zealand in 1953.

Having been given the afternoon off school to witness a Royal visit to Hastings, East Sussex in June 1997, 13-year-old Amberley Walker found herself warming to 'the nation's grandmother'.

66 Her Majesty was opening the new Priory Meadow shopping centre in Hastings. Most of the town had lined the streets to see The Queen and the Duke of Edinburgh. I joined a small group from my school in the Old Town, where we stood waving Union Jacks. We stood for some time before her car arrived, followed by her entourage including her lady-in-waiting.

The Queen walked along the rows of people, stopping every so often to say hello. When she came to our little group, she stopped to greet us. She asked if the school had given us the afternoon off lessons to see her, which we told her had been the case. 'How lovely!' she replied before moving on. Two things stick in my head about that meeting. One is just how tiny she was, her clothes were beautiful and her hair set – she looked like a little doll. The second is that whilst she was speaking to us, I noticed that she had cerise pink lipstick on, some of which was on her teeth! I wondered why her lady-in-waiting had not been more observant! Before this encounter I had an image of The Queen as being a little cold; but on the contrary, she appeared to be a very sweet lady. Not unlike any normal grandmother she came across as very natural and down to earth, I was very impressed. 99

WINDSOR, ENGLAND
14 JUNE 1999

The Queen at the Garter Ceremony. The order was founded in 1348 by Edward III after Joan, Countess of Salisbury, dropped her garter at a court ball and the King picked it up, rebuking his sniggering courtiers by saying *Honi soit qui mal y pense* (meaning 'evil [or shame] be to him who thinks ill of it'), which remains the motto of the Order to this day.

As Chief of Protocol for the Province of New Brunswick, Anne Reynolds was in charge of organizing The Queen's Golden Jubilee tour to the Province, planning for which began two years before the visit.

" Although Her Majesty's visit was just a little over 24 hours, her programme was very ambitious, allowing her to visit Fredericton (the provincial capital), Sussex, Moncton and the Francophone community of Dieppe and to attend numerous events and meet hundreds of New Brunswickers. The weather was absolutely perfect – sunny with breathtaking fall foliage. There were thousands of people lining the streets along the route from the airport and thousands more waiting for her arrival at Old Government House. It was a magical visit and extremely moving, and the looks of people's faces when Her Majesty stopped to speak to people were really incredible.

One of the highlights of the visit for me occurred during my private audience with Her Majesty and the Duke of Edinburgh, at which time Her Majesty made me a Lieutenant of the Royal Victorian Order. I was so overwhelmed that I am not sure I even remembered to curtsey. I do remember that I started to leave the room through the wrong door and that the Duke kindly pointed me in the right direction. "

JASPER, CANADA
22 MAY 2005

The Queen on a walkabout outside St Mary and St George Church during her private retreat in Jasper. The town of Jasper is named after Jasper Hawes, a clerk with the North West Company which, early in the 19th century, established Jasper House close to what is now the eastern edge of Jasper National Park.

When model Linda Peek went out looking for work she did not expect an assignment from Norman Hartnell, or to be modelling for The Queen.

"In early autumn 1963, with a new portfolio of photographs under my arm, I was doing the usual trek around the West End delivering composite sheets to hundreds of photographic studios. This was the third day and I was tired, depressed and my feet hurt. I found myself in Bruton Street next to Norman Hartnell's salon and decided to just walk in and ask for a job. I was lucky – the big man was there! He looked me over and asked me to walk around the room, then he said, 'Be back here at 2.30pm and for goodness sake do something with that hair! I'll decide then.' On my way out he shouted after me, 'Can you curtsey?' I replied that I could, though I'd never curtsied in my life.

I spent £3.00 having my hair done and returned promptly at 2.30. Three other girls were in the model room and we were dressed in fabulous gowns. Mine was blue organza with the Hartnell trademark of jewels down the front and around the hem. Two minutes before the viewing we were told that The Queen was present with two ladies-in-waiting. Frantically we practised our curtsies! It went well and when it was my turn I did my curtsey and smiled directly at The Queen. She returned my smile and asked with a laugh, 'Doesn't that itch?' I laughed and said, 'No Ma'am, it's made of very soft organza.' 'Lovely', she then said and I curtsied again and left the platform. I got the job!"

BONN, GERMANY
19 OCTOBER 1992

The Queen attends a State banquet at Schloss Augustusburg on the first night of her State visit to Germany, her first official visit to Germany since reunification.

TAUNTON, ENGLAND
2 MAY 2002

The Queen visits the farmers' market at Vivary Park, Taunton, on the second day of her
Golden Jubilee Tour of the UK. Vivary Park is so-called because it occupies the site of the fish
farm, or vivarium, that once supplied the local priory and castle.

LONDON, ENGLAND
4 AUGUST 1999

The Queen and Princess Margaret outside Clarence House
on the occasion of The Queen Mother's 99th birthday.

When Audrey Haynes (née Carter) was drafted into the Women's Royal Canadian Naval Service, she little expected that she would later find herself singing sea shanties with Princess Elizabeth, later HM Queen Elizabeth II.

"" While I was serving in the Women's Royal Canadian Naval Service I had an experience of a lifetime. Wren May Dickinson and I had visited Girl Guide headquarters in London and went on to receive an invitation to attend a Sea Ranger meeting at Windsor Castle on Friday, 6 April 1945. The highlight of our visit was being introduced to Princess Elizabeth in her Sea Ranger uniform and Princess Margaret in her Girl Guide uniform. I gave them my best naval salute, followed by a Girl Guide handshake. Each visitor had a Sea Ranger as a guide for a tour of the castle and, as luck would have it, Princess Margaret, seeing that I had been left alone by my guide, offered to stay with me for the rest of the evening.

Around the campfire Princess Elizabeth led us in a sea shanty. The other war guests sang their countries' songs and the Canadians chose, as was only natural, 'Land of the Silver Birch'. It was a perfect evening. When we waiting for the train to go home the 'Skipper' thanked us for remembering that a Girl Guide meeting was one of the few places that the Princesses could relax and enjoy themselves. ""

SANDRINGHAM, ENGLAND
28 DECEMBER 1985

The Queen attends a Christmas church service in the snow on a bitterly cold day at Sandringham.

ABUJA, NIGERIA
5 DECEMBER 2003

Aiden Modebe (six) gives a deep bow to The Queen, to the obvious delight of Her Majesty and all the onlookers. Robin Nunn remembers: 'He took us all by surprise because it was just a routine visit to the British Council offices and he stole the show with the best bow of all time!'

PRETORIA, SOUTH AFRICA
10 NOVEMBER 1999

The Queen arrives for a State banquet hosted by
President and Mrs Mbeki at the Presidential Guest House.

OPPOSITE PAGE

CALGARY, CANADA
25 MAY 2005

The Queen bids farewell to Canada on the last day of her
2005 visit – an emotional moment amid rumours that this
would be her last major foreign tour.

OTTAWA, CANADA
13 OCTOBER 2002

The Queen arrives in the rain for a thanksgiving celebration on Parliament
Hill, wearing a rock crystal and diamond brooch that she had given to her
mother on The Queen Mother's 100th birthday.

ST ALBANS, ENGLAND
14 MARCH 2003

The Queen at St Albans Cathedral, where a theatrical
display by local schoolchildren meets with royal approval.

ABUJA, NIGERIA
5 DECEMBER 2003

The Queen leads a toast to the Commonwealth at a
Commonwealth Heads of Government meeting in the Nigerian capital.

Until his retirement in 2005, Christopher Samuels had for 22 years been Rector of St Mary Without-the-Walls, Chester, and for four years been Canon of Chester Cathedral and Chaplain to The Queen. He recalls two of the occasions on which he met Her Majesty.

66 On 12 May 2004, The Queen kindly invited her Chaplains to Hampton Court Palace for a service in the Chapel and lunch afterwards to celebrate the 400th anniversary of the authorisation of the Bible by King James I on exactly the same day in 1604. The Queen's strong sense of history, and her understanding of the importance of authorising the Bible throughout the land at that time, came across in the service and during lunch. It was particularly good that Prince Philip read the lesson from one of the few remaining copies of this Bible and that, together with The Queen, we were able to look at and hold this copy. During lunch The Queen mingled with her Chaplains, genuinely enjoying conversations about the Anniversary and recognising how it marked an historic moment in the life of the nation. She was able to maintain a balance between the seriousness of the occasion and its celebratory nature. This is one of her great strengths. 99

The Queen waves to onlookers during an awayday to Cambridge, where she unveiled a plaque to commemorate both the 500th anniversary of the foundation of Christ's College and her own visit with the Duke of Edinburgh, who is Chancellor of the University of Cambridge.

ACCRA, GHANA
8 NOVEMBER 1999

The Queen during a three-day State visit to Ghana.

PARIS, FRANCE
5 APRIL 2004

The Queen, the Duke of Edinburgh, and President and Mrs Chirac meet Aga Khan III
at a State banquet at the Elysée Palace on the first night of her three-day State visit to
France to celebrate the 100th anniversary of the most recent revival of *entente cordiale*.

As one of the world's leading wildlife artists, an internationally renowned conservationist, and portrait painter to luminaries including Kenneth Kaunda and The Queen Mother, David Shepherd, OBE, is no stranger to State occasions – but one memory stands out from the rest.

" The first President of the Republic of Zambia was Dr Kenneth Kaunda, and because of his interest in conservation we became close personal friends. On a State visit to London, therefore, my wife Avril and I were asked to a State banquet at Buckingham Palace. Being staunch monarchists and supporters of everything British, we were thrilled to be asked to such an event. When the final moment came to meet the line-up of Royals, we were very excited. Our turn came to be announced, 'Ma'am, Mr and Mrs David Shepherd'. I had only met The Queen very briefly on a couple of previous occasions, but I will never forget her amazing memory, almost like an encyclopedia, greeting people as though she knew them well. I bowed to her Majesty, she turned to President Kaunda and said one word, 'Elephants'. 'Yes, I know, Ma'am', said President Kaunda. We will both treasure that memory for ever. "

BANDAR SERI BEGAWAN, BRUNEI
18 SEPTEMBER 1998

The Queen in the capital of Brunei on the second day of her State visit.

MAPUTO, MOZAMBIQUE
15 NOVEMBER 1999

The Queen at a State banquet in Mozambique's capital Maputo, which until 1975
was known as Lourenço Marques. Having been a Marxist one-party state
until 1990, Mozambique was admitted to the Commonwealth in November 1995
because of its close ties with other African Commonwealth countries.

WINDSOR, ENGLAND
13 MAY 2000

The Queen watching the Duke of Edinburgh driving a carriage in the International Driving
Grand Prix (IDGP) at the Royal Windsor Horse Show, an event first introduced in 1970. The
Duke won the IDGP Horse Teams Event in 1982 and the IDGP Pony Teams Class in 1989.

Twelve-year-old Meghan Hines and her dog Quixote were overjoyed to meet The Queen when she visited Toronto – and provided Canadian Lions dog trainers with a new benchmark for discipline.

" At the Festival of Ontario my service dog, Quixote, and I had the opportunity to participate in an exhibit of working dogs. Quixote, a white standard poodle, is a Special Skills Dog who was specially trained and paired with me in 1999. I have muscular dystrophy and use a wheelchair and Quixote helps me with daily living activities, such as opening doors, turning on lights, picking up things, and so much more.

Throughout the course of the evening, Her Majesty toured the exhibits. When she arrived at where I was, I presented her with a basket of flowers. I was extremely nervous – anybody would be, she is The Queen of England! Her Majesty was very kind and gracious and interested in our exhibit as there were over 15 dogs of all types present, and I know she really likes dogs.

Later a man came up to me, started talking to me, and reached over to pet Quixote. Because Quixote was working I had to tell the man he couldn't pet him. The man respected this, and went on his way. My dad chuckled and asked me if I knew who the man was. I told him 'no', and he informed me that he was Prince Philip, the Duke of Edinburgh! Ever since then, the trainers at the Lions Foundation of Canada have told this story to new service dog owners to reinforce the fact that no one gets to pet your service dog while it is working – not even the Duke of Edinburgh! "

TORONTO, CANADA
9 OCTOBER 2002

The Queen at the Festival of Ontario, a special celebration of Ontario's
culture held in the National Trade Centre in the province's capital, Toronto.

The Queen attends a remembrance service in Durban during a visit
to South Africa for a Commonwealth Heads of Government meeting.

ACCRA, GHANA
8 NOVEMBER 1999

The Queen meets tribal chiefs and their wives at a durbar, or festival of welcome.

Marlene McCracken was born three months before Her Majesty's Coronation in 1953. Having joined The Monarchist League of Canada in 1981, she became the Kingston, Ontario, Branch Chairman in 2002, since when she has organised an annual community tea in honour of The Queen's birthday.

❝ In 1973 my summer job took me to Ottawa, where I was hired by the House of Commons to work in the Library of Parliament. You can imagine my excitement when I learned that The Queen would be unveiling a plaque in front of the library. Those working for the House of Commons lined up, five people deep, on the left side of the hallway in order to watch the event. I was short in stature and had ended up in the back row behind a man over six-feet tall. A security guard tapped me on the shoulder and marched me over to the right side of the hall where the Senate staff were only one person deep. This dear man, knowing my enthusiasm for the Monarchy, ignored my comments that I worked for the House of Commons not the Senate. When the procession arrived, Her Majesty stopped and greeted those on the Senate side, shaking hands and saying a brief word. I was ready to curtsey, but when Her Majesty arrived in front of me I froze, my knees locked and I looked like a deer caught in car headlights. May Her Gracious Majesty grant me humble forgiveness for not showing the respect our Queen deserved. ❞

OTTAWA, CANADA
15 OCTOBER 2002

A Royal wave goodbye at the end of The Queen's
Golden Jubilee visit to Canada.

ACKNOWLEDGEMENTS

PHOTOGRAPHY

Taking the pictures is the easy part in a project like *Happy & Glorious* as it is behind the scenes that the real hard work is done and I'm so fortunate that my colleagues in this, and many other ventures, are the best in the business. Aasta Børte is not only an exceptional Royal photographer in her own right, but her ability to recall key images and moments is unique and mesmerizing and was absolutely essential to the picture research required for the book. David Porter patiently managed the administration of the project from start to finish and Adam Tudor from Carter-Ruck firmly ensured that our legal and IPR interest were protected throughout.

ROBIN NUNN
London, November 2005

TEXT

With special thanks to Terry Guillon (Chief of the Canadian Parliamentary Press Gallery) for providing a wealth of information for the captions, based on the flimsiest of starting-points, and to Yorkshire correspondent Phil Harrison for his tireless efforts in tracing northerners who have met the Queen. Thanks also to the following people and organisations for their help in researching *Happy & Glorious*: John Aimers, Caroline Allen, Philip Benwell, Nicholas Bond, Craig Chouinard, Noel Cox, Emma Danby (Buckingham Palace Press Office), Danielle di Michiel, Patricia Green, Alpha Hopkins, Michael Jackson, Harish Chandar Jain, Joe Little, Jamie Mackay (www.nzhistory.net.nz), Lt-Col. Sean O'Dwyer, Bill Rennells, Michael Richards, Rosemary Rowe, Susie Schofield, Chris Vezey, Geraldine Voost (www.etoile.co.uk), Robert Warholm of The British Royalty Message Board, BBC Information, New Zealand Ministry for Culture and Heritage, Old Parliament House (ACT, Australia), Robert Elms Show (BBC London 94.9 FM), Royal Agricultural Benevolent Institution, Royal National Lifeboat Institution, Saga Radio, The Australian Monarchist League, The Monarchist League of Canada, The Monarchist League of New Zealand.

IAN HARRISON
London, November 2005

The publisher would like to thank Ian Harrison for his extremely hard work, persistence, and unflagging enthusiasm in researching and compiling the accounts used in this book, John Round for his design work and Gabrielle Mander for getting the project off the ground.

Note: While Cassell Illustrated have made every reasonable effort to contact copyright holders and to obtain permission for the reproduction of the accounts in this book, this has not been possible in all cases. However, where any omissions have been made we shall, if informed by the copyright holder, be happy to insert the appropriate credit for future editions.